CHRISTMAS
Coloring Book

This Book Belongs To:

....

Want FREEBIES?

100 FREE COLORING PAGES

Email Us At:

eightidd@gmail.com

Title the email "Coloring Book Kids" and let us know that you purchased our book.

THANKS FOR YOUR AMAZING SUPPORT!

>>>>>>>>>>>>>>>>>>>>>>>>>>>>>>>>>>>>>

For Enquiries and Customer Service email us at:

eightidd@gmail.com

Sample Pages

We create all of our books with love and care. If you want to find more Coloring Books like this one,

SCAN THE OR CODE BELLOW

>>>>>>>>>>>>>>>>>>>>>>>>>>>>>>>>>>>>>>

We don't exist without you. A brief review could help us a lot. Please leave your feedback about this book.

Merry
CHRISTMAS !

Merry
CHRISTMAS !

Merry
CHRISTMAS !

Merry CHRISTMAS !

Merry CHRISTMAS !

Merry CHRISTMAS !

Merry CHRISTMAS !

Merry CHRISTMAS !

Merry CHRISTMAS !

Merry
CHRISTMAS !

Merry CHRISTMAS !

Merry
CHRISTMAS !

Merry
CHRISTMAS !

Merry CHRISTMAS !

Merry CHRISTMAS !

Merry
CHRISTMAS !

Merry CHRISTMAS !

Merry
CHRISTMAS !

Merry CHRISTMAS !

Merry
CHRISTMAS !

Merry CHRISTMAS !

Merry CHRISTMAS !

Merry CHRISTMAS !

Merry
CHRISTMAS !

Merry
CHRISTMAS !

Merry
CHRISTMAS !

Merry CHRISTMAS !

Merry CHRISTMAS !

Merry CHRISTMAS !

Merry
CHRISTMAS !

Merry CHRISTMAS !

Merry CHRISTMAS !

Merry CHRISTMAS !

Merry
CHRISTMAS !

Merry
CHRISTMAS !

Merry CHRISTMAS !

Merry
CHRISTMAS !

Merry
CHRISTMAS !

Merry CHRISTMAS !

Merry
CHRISTMAS !

Merry
CHRISTMAS !

Merry
CHRISTMAS !

Merry CHRISTMAS !

Merry CHRISTMAS !

Merry
CHRISTMAS !

Merry
CHRISTMAS !

Merry
CHRISTMAS !

Merry CHRISTMAS !

Merry CHRISTMAS !

Merry CHRISTMAS !

Merry CHRISTMAS !

Made in the USA
Monee, IL
17 November 2021